# ZERO GRAVITY

# Books by Gwyneth Lewis

POETRY IN ENGLISH

*Parables & Faxes* (Bloodaxe Books, 1995)
*Zero Gravity* (Bloodaxe Books, 1998)

POETRY IN WELSH

*Sonedau Redsa* (Gwasg Gomer, 1990)
*Cyfrif Un ac Un yn Dri* (Cyhoeddiadau Barddas, 1996)

# GWYNETH LEWIS

# ZERO GRAVITY

## BLOODAXE BOOKS

ISBN: 1 85224 456 9

First published 1998 by
Bloodaxe Books Ltd,
P.O. Box 1SN,
Newcastle upon Tyne NE99 1SN.

Bloodaxe Books Ltd acknowledges
the financial assistance of Northern Arts.

Cover printing by J. Thomson Colour Printers Ltd, Glasgow.

Printed in Great Britain by
Cromwell Press Ltd, Trowbridge, Wiltshire.

*To Leighton*

# Acknowledgements

Acknowledgements are due to the editors of the following publications in which some of these poems first appeared: *The Atlanta Review* (USA), *Drawing Down the Moon* (Seren, 1996), *The Express, Making for Planet Alice* (Bloodaxe Books, 1997), *Metre* (Prague), *New Writing 5* (Viking, 1996), *Pivot* (USA), *PN Review, Poetry Review, Poetry Wales, The Printer's Devil, Quadrant* (Australia), *The Sunday Times* and *The Times Literary Supplement*.

*The Mind Museum* was commissioned by Fiet and set to music by John Metcalf. The work was first performed by the BBC National Orchestra of Wales at St David's Hall in Cardiff on 29 March 1998. The version published here is slightly revised.

The opening of 'Soul Candles' is based on a line from Thomas Traherne. The first two lines of 'Will and the Wall' are the translation of a Welsh saying. The epigraph to *Zero Gravity* is from *Space Facts* by Caroline Stott and Clint Twist (Dorling Kindersley, 1995); the quotation is taken from page 13.

I would like to thank Elizabeth Fairbairn, Herb Leibowitz and Les Murray for their interest and sound advice.

# Contents

# 1   ZERO GRAVITY

# ZERO GRAVITY

## A Space Requiem

*In memory of my sister-in-law*
*Jacqueline Badham*
(1944-1997)

*and to commemorate the voyage of my cousin*
*Joe Tanner and the crew of Space Shuttle STS-82*
*to repair the Hubble Space Telescope*
*(February 1997)*

*'The easiest way to think of the universe is as a sphere which is constantly expanding so that everything is getting farther away from everything else.'*

SPACE FACTS

# I PROLOGUE

We watched you go
in glory: Shuttle,
comet, sister-in-law.

The one came back.
The other two
went further. Love's an attack

on time. The whole damn thing
explodes, leaving
us with our count-down days

still more than zero.
My theme is change.
My point of view

ecstatic. See how speed
transforms us? Didn't you know
that time's a fiction? We don't need

it for travel. Distance
is a matter of seeing;
faith, a science

of feeling faint objects.
Of course, this is no
consolation as we watch you go

on your dangerous journeys.
This out of mind
hurts badly when you're left behind.

Don't leave us.
We have more to say
before the darkness. Don't go. Stay

a little longer. But you're out of reach
already. Above us the sky
sees with its trillion trillion eyes.

## II

Day one at the Wakulla Beach Motel.
There are sixty of us here for the launch.
The kids have found lizards down by the pool,
been shopping in Ron Jon's. I mooch
and admire new body boards. My afternoon's
spent watching them surfing. The sea's my skirt,
breakers my petticoat. Along the seams
of rollers I watch cousins fall without getting hurt
as pelicans button the evening's blouse
into the rollers. The brothers wait,
each head a planet in the shallows' blaze.
They're blind to all others, are a constella-
tion whose gravity makes them surge forward, race
one another, arms flailing, for the broken spume
where they rise, bodies burnished, run back to the place
agreed on for jumping. They laugh in the foam
and I see eclipses, ellipses in the seethe
of a brash outer space. But here they can breathe.

**III**

It looks like she's drowning
in a linen tide.
They bring babies like cameras
to her bedside

because they can't see dying.
She looks too well
to be leaving. She listens
to anecdotes we tell –

how we met and got married.
She recounts a story:
her friend went stark mad
carrying, feeding, bleeding – all three

at once. She tried to bury
herself in Barry Island sand.
Her prayer plant has flowered
after seven years. She sends

Robert to fetch it from System St.
She thinks a bee sting
started the cancer.
We can't say a thing.

IV

Bored early morning down on Cocoa Beach,
the kids build castles. I know my history,
so after they've heaped up their Norman keep
(with flags of seaweed) I draw Caerphilly's
concentric fortress. Five-year-old Mary,
who's bringing us shells as they come to hand,
announces, surprised: 'I am the boss of me.'
She has a centre. In our busy sand
we throw up ramparts, a ring of walls
which Sarah crenellates. Being self-contained
can be very stylish – we plan boiling oil!
But soon we're in trouble with what we've designed.
So much for our plans to be fortified.
Our citadel falls to a routine tide.

## V

First time I saw the comet, I finally knew
that I'd always love him. I watched it go,

dead starlight headed for a dying sun
then away into darkness. It was gone

before we knew what its brilliance meant,
a human moment in immense

spirals of nothing. I feel his pull
in my blood salts. The comet's tail

is a searchlight from another point,
and the point is once you've given your heart

there are no replacements. Oh, your soul,
if that can escape from its own black hole.

Last suppers, I fancy, are always wide-screen.
I see this one in snapshot: your brothers are rhymes
with you and each other. John has a shiner
from surfing. Already we've started counting time
backwards to zero. The Shuttle processed
out like an idol to its pagan pad.
It stands by its scaffold, being tended and blessed
by priestly technicians. You refuse to feel sad,
can't wait for your coming wedding with speed
out into weightlessness. We watch you dress
in your orange space suit, a Hindu bride,
with wires like henna for your loveliness.
You carry your helmet like a severed head.
We think of you as already dead.

# VII

Her voyage is inwards.
Now looking back
is a matter of passing events.
She makes for the dark

of not being human.
In turn she recalls
giving birth to Robert;
further back, a fall

while pregnant, the bathroom floor
of slate that saved her.
Silk parachute dresses
just after the war.

A bay tree, a garden, Victoria plums.
Then nothing before the age of ten
when a man attacked her.
It must be that pain

accelerates something.
Her speeding mind
leaves us in the present,
a long way behind.

## VIII

Thousands arrive when a bird's about to fly,
crowding the causeways. 'Houston. Weather is a go
and counting.' I pray for you as you lie
on your back facing upwards. A placard shows
local, Shuttle and universal time.
Numbers run out. Zero always comes.
'Main engines are gimballed' and I'm
not ready for this, but clouds of steam
billow out sideways and a sudden spark
lifts the rocket on a collective roar
that comes from inside us. With a sonic crack
the spaceship explodes to a flower of fire
on the scaffold's stamen. We sob and swear,
helpless, but we're lifting a sun
with our love's attention, we hear
the Shuttle's death rattle as it overcomes
its own weight with glory, setting car alarms
off in the Keys and then it's gone
out of this time zone, into the calm
of black and we've lost the lemon dawn
your vanishing made. At the viewing site
we pick oranges for your missing light.

## IX

The day before
she went she said
'Nothing matters.'
Now that she's dead

she's wiped herself off
our neural screens.
We no longer reach her.
But Jacqueline –

not her body,
nor her history,
nor our view of her –
now she's free

of her rubbish,
explodes on the eye
that perceives faint objects
on an inner sky.

She's our supernova,
sends joyous light
out of her ending.
To our delight

we fell neutrinos
from her ruined core,
can't take our eyes
off her stunning star.

# X

Drew trips over his shadow by the pool
but picks himself up. We keep TVs on
like memorial flames, listen as Mission Control
gives cool instructions You are a sun
we follow, tracking your time over Africa,
a fauvist desert. We see you fall
past pointillist clouds in the Bahamas,
past glaciers, silent hurricanes, the Nile.
We're all provincials when it comes to maps
so we look out for Florida. The world's a road
above you – but you have no 'up',
only an orbit as you dive towards
an opal Pacific, now you see dawn
every ninety minutes. The Shuttle's a cliff
that's shearing, you on it, every way's 'down',
vertiginous plunging. It is yourself
you hold on to, till you lose your grip
on that, even. Then your soul's the ship.

## XI

The second time the comet swung by
the knife went deeper. It hissed through the sky

like phosphorus on water. It marked a now,
an only-coming-once, a this-ness we knew

we'd keep forgetting. Its vapour trails
mimicked our voyage along ourselves,

our fire with each other, the endless cold
which surrounds that burning. Don't be fooled

by fireworks. It's no accident that *leave*
fails but still tries to rhyme with *love*.

## XII

Only your eyesight can be used in space.
Now you've captured the telescope, nebulae
are birthmarks on your new-born face.
The sun's flare makes a Cyclops eye
on your visor. The new spectrograph
you've installed in the Hubble to replace the old
makes black holes leap closer, allows us to grasp
back in time through distance, to see stars unfold
in nuclear gardens, galaxies like sperm
swirled in water, rashes of young hot stars,
blood-clot catastrophes, febrile swarms
of stinging explosions. But what's far
doesn't stop hurting. Give me a gaze
that sees deep into systems through clouds of debris
to the heart's lone pulsar, let me be amazed
by the red shifts, the sheer luminosity
that plays all around us as we talk on the beach,
thinking there's nothing between us but speech.

# XIII

What is her vanishing point?
Now that she's dead
but still close by
we assume she's heard

our conversations.
Out of sight? Out of mind?
On her inward journey
she's travelled beyond

the weight of remembering.
The g-force lifts
from her labouring chest.
Forgetting's a gift

of lightness. She's sped
vast distances
already, she's shed
her many bodies –

cancer, hope, regard,
marriage, forgiving.
Get rid of time
and everything's dancing,

forget straight lines,
all's blown away.
Now's honey from the bees of night,
music from the bees of day.

There are great advantages to having been dead.
They say that Lazarus never laughed again,
but I doubt it. Your space suit was a shroud
and at night you slept in a catacomb,
posed like a statue. So, having been
out to infinity, you experienced the heat
and roar of re-entry, blood in the veins
then, like a baby, had to find your feet
under you, stagger with weight, learn to cope
again with gravity. Next came the tour
of five states with a stopover in Europe.
You let people touch you, told what you saw.
This counts as a death and a second birth
within one lifetime. This point of view
is radical, its fruit must be mirth
at one's own unimportance and now, although
you're famous, a "someone", you might want much less.
Your laughter's a longing for weightlessness.

# XV

Last sight of the comet. The sky's a screen
riddled with pinpricks, hung in between

me and what happened – a room not quite
hidden from me. Hale-Bopp's light

says something dazzling's taking place beyond,
involving moving. My mind

is silver nitrate, greedy for form
but I fail to grasp it here in this gloom.

Memory's a crude camera.
I wish you were seared on my retina

so I was blind to anything less
than your leaving. But the darkness

is kind. Dawn will heal with colour
my grief for your self-consuming core.

A neighbourhood party
to welcome you home
from the Shuttle's tomb.

It's a wake in sunshine –
kids dive-bomb the pool.
My sense of scale's

exploded. Now I wear
glass beads like planets.
In my ears

are quasars. I have meteorites
for a bracelet, a constellation
necklace so bright

that, despite dark matter
in the heart,
I'm dazzled. 'Here' and 'there'

have flared together. A nonchalant father
throws Saturn rings.
Dive for them now and find everything.

# II  COCONUT POSTCARDS

## Coconut Postcards

*A Goan Honeymoon*


### I

Wrapped in the palm trees' parentheses
the peninsula sighs. The repeated Vs
rustle of rain to come, but not tonight...
One tree is everything to us – is food, is light,
shelter and matting, drunkenness and shade,
boat or a ladder. We use it shamelessly –
eating it, plaiting it, as though it were made
solely for us, and still it gives more.
It's rooted in loving and has no fear
of its own exhaustion. Note how its star
is an asterisk: something important is planted here.


### II

'You can have all the one-night stands you want
with me once we're married.' Along the waterfront
bee-eaters squeal as they strip the air
of its writing of insects; seagulls pilfer
wrist-watch crabs from the clock of the sea
which tells us our time. Like a silver boat
the moon has set sail on the light that we
must take as our monument today,
for we've married each other's dying. We pay
the ferryman's fare as he poles his way
past porpoise rip-tides in the darkening bay.

III

Back in his Sanskrit childhood, when a pile of stones
was a god, the Contractor was never alone,
was pantheistic. Now his head's a Kali
fixed to the sway of an avenger's body
in a ruined temple – a pose he holds for the wife.
He refuses to swim because of jellyfish,
which disgust him. He has lived a life
of thrust, of direction, he is a man of spine,
despising drift. But he fears the sting
of the floating organ, whose transparent design
can kill him by willing nothing.

IV

Entombed on their towels, the honeymooners gleam...
Alabaster limbs and gothic dreams
keep waiters away, for they lie in state.
Burnished by unguents they concentrate
on just being, now that all their delights
are formal, official. So their smiles are fixed –
eyes closed to the wheeling Brahminy kites
above, to the life around them, to the dissolute
hibiscus tongues, to the siren's alarms
as a baby's found buried in a palm tree's roots,
re-born from the earth into fostering arms.

## V

Palm number eight is a toddy-tapping tree,
is fortunate, owns a family
which tends to its every need. In return
it allows them to place a strategic urn
over its sweetly bleeding stem
so that Polycarp d'Souza's still
is full. All night the palm tree bleeds for them.
At noon, girls gather in its fertile shade,
striped like tigers, for their husbandry's
ferocious – best marriage a tree could have made
against its main enemy, gravity.


## VI

By the shack a man wants to clean out my ears
and then massage me. In the end I concur
and settle my lug-hole so that he can reach
its whorls. He digs and suddenly the beach
is louder. He picks out detritus, wax and more –
out comes a string of my memories –
leaving me light in the midday roar
of sand grains crashing and singing crabs. I'm
relieved of all the rubbish I've ever heard,
re-tuned, a transistor that can hear the first time
the call of the heart's hidden weaver-bird.

## VII

On the beach you can practise our history
and crawl, amphibian, up from the sea
then under umbrellas to be something cool
in shorts and dark glasses. Look quizzical
as the sea's empty metre sighs at the feet
of a palm that carries flowers, acorns, fruit
all the same moment. At dusk we're freed
from shape into colour. On an opal tide
we swim: skin opens into lilacs and far
below the tuna's silver shoots through my side.
I reach out my tongue and lick Africa.


## VIII

This place, like paradise, is better than us
but accepts us graciously, puts us at ease
with love's broad tolerance, so kind
that it only condemns the begrudging mind,
which exiles itself. For the moment, my dear,
simplification's the name of the game.
Set me up slowly like a folding chair
in the sun and, serenely, let's look out together
at the scenery and common life
which bless us repeatedly in the insect stir
of a palm-frond husband with his sea-breeze wife.

# The Love of Furniture

### I

I think today I'll wear my dresser,
the oak one with my grandmother's

china, the set her father bought for her
in Aberystwyth. I fancy lustrewear

and cake plates. Royal Albert's the future
of punk. Not everyone has hardwood to wear,

a set of brass-handled drawers.
But I have inheritance. So there.

## II

I dreamt about us last night, my dear.
You were a wardrobe. Behind your doors

hung velvet dresses, satin shirts,
wet-look raincoats, watered-silk skirts

scented with lemon. You offered me more
than I'd ever dared to want before

and were capacious. So I picked out
a soft, well-tailored, shimmering suit

that sat just so then I made my way
out through the door and into the day.

**III**

The sofa bride is a pair of hips
for two to sit on. Upholstered lips

are plumped-up for love. She is a *chaise*
he yearns to be *longue* on. A promiscuous phase

has been polished over, a cabriole limb
that was gymnastic, restored to be prim,

fit for one owner. She'll take the strain
of his violence. Later he'll claim

that she tricked him, that they married too soon.
Settees with a past shouldn't wish for the moon.

IV

In battle all men shall remember
never to endanger the Admiral's furniture

on pain of death. It is essential
that the commander's gate-legged table

be stowed in the hold. It is worth far more
than the chap who made her. In times of war

chattels come first. If the hold is full
and the orlop deck cluttered with terrible

bodies then, seamen, be sure to launch a boat
and fill it with hautboy and with sideboard

for the enemy has agreed not to fire
on his fixtures and fittings. For, to be fair,

which of you can say that you've shown
such loyalty to a man of renown

or such service as his china and silver?
Lord Nelson's desk? Lord Nelson's easy chair?

V

There have been tales of great self-sacrifice
on the part of furniture. Take that chest of drawers

in the Kōbe earthquake. When the building fell
it flung itself down the tumbling stairwell

across its mistress who, pregnant, lay trapped
in the rubble for days. Its rosewood back

took the strain of girders. Its sturdiness
became her pelvis, allowed her to press

down on her daughter, helped her give birth
out of pulverised concrete and earth

by marquetry's artifice. Those dovetailed joints
gave life to another, though the effort meant

total collapse once the rescuers came
with shawls and shovels, ruined the frame

that had saved the baby. Now, once a year
on a certain date a woman and daughter

visit the grave on a building site
where fine wood was burnt. Lest they forget.

# The Booming Bittern

Listen to that bittern boom.
You'll never see him. Tall reeds sway
and so does he,
courting invisibility.
Boom, bittern, boom.

See, he points up to the sky
in sympathy with wind-stirred sedge.
He has a body
but his camouflage
has made this bird all alibi.

This discretion's saved his life
so far. He sways in silence but he'll die
alone. The boom's
his only hope – his cry
might bring a brood of chicks, a wife.

To boom or not? A car alarm
risks nothing when it calls its mate.
But in a bog
you must be found, or not copulate.
So risk it, bittern. Boom, bittern, boom!

# Good Dog!

All pets are part of one animal.
They look out at us from domestic eyes
hoping for food and a little love.
People who believe in reincarnation
feel the concern of departed relatives
shine from the heart of new-born pups,
so confide in them, spoil them.
A well-placed '*Om*' in a mongrel's ear
can save the soul of a dying dog.

Ours is theologian. He knows
that sticks in life are more reliable than cats
and that balls are better. Everything thrown
is instantly precious, well worth running for.
The river he loves and tends to wear
it often. A Baptist, he immerses himself
with total abandon so his otter soul
is renewed in the feeder with the bags of crisps
and ribbons of algae.
He wears the medal of himself with joy.

Something there is about a dog
draws conversation from frosty men
and available women. Trick for lonely boys and girls:
Get a dog. Walk him. For be it ugly or pure-bred,
a dog on a lead says: 'Here is a love
that makes its bargain with bad habits and smells,
the brute in a person, can accommodate needs
far other than its own, allows for beastliness.'

Some nights our lodger gets his favourite ball,
runs into the river and tramples the moon.

# Peripheral Vision

### I

Not everyone sees it, but I glimpsed the man
inside our terrier. We'd walked up the lane,
he stood back, a second, to let me in

through the gate, so courtly that, on my inner eye,
I saw him for the first time clearly
not a dog but a dish dressed in soft chamois,

tall like a prince, with thigh-length boots.
I said I would marry him. Sepia street lights
were our veil as, with love, I opened the locks

to our royal dwelling. Then, back on all fours,
he was wagging his tail by the kitchen door.
Beauty hides in the beast. This is the law.

## II *The gods still walk around South Wales*

Caught in a traffic jam outside the Monico
cinema, a girl called idly on Apollo,
not meaning it. A stranger steps in. 'We'll go

up to the Beacons,' he said. 'I am
the answer to your prayers, a dangerous man,
not *deus ex machina* but lunatic in van.'

So she drove, directed by his Stanley knife,
fearing now for her hairdresser life
on B roads, till he'd ravished her enough

in lay-bys, near beauty-spot streams
to satisfy her kidnap dreams.
They say she made it all up. But how come

her joy, despite all the names she was called
by hacks and her neighbours? How come she recalled
such transport of love, a shower of gold?

III  *View from an ocean-going liner*

Of course the poet Juan Ramón Jiménez
saw the sirens sink into mercury seas
off the coast of America. A disease

of the literal meant that his eyes
could focus on metaphor. Manatees
were mermaids. The Furies

came later. Once such figures are in the frame
you're finished. The way things seem is no longer home.
Sirens never stopped singing for him.

# III  THE SOUL CANDLE

# Soul Candles

I will
by the light
of my tinder soul
show you
the universe.

\*

My hair's in streamers
of scorching air.
My mother stands over me
brushing my mane,
trying to tame it.
The plait explodes,
sloughs off to darkness
in roils of flame
fed on oils
of abandon.
My face is the same
under the roaring,
unravelling skeins.
I've plenty of tallow,
will burn a long time.

\*

His revenge was ironic:
us two in the car
doused down with petrol,
one flick of a lighter
and everything's changed.
But his hate
brought us closer.
He gave us this,
deep in the sinews:
now that we share
the nerve ends' scorching,

our mutual heat
is a marriage,
this burning unbearable
but conjugal night.

\*

His fierce bolt
keeps happening.
Even my veins
are made for his lightning.
I search for his volts
in stillness.
Soul's bright kite
tugs on its string,
nudging for danger,
for ruinous strike.

\*

After the light show
which, from afar
was spectacular,
comes the real burning.
If you care
for me, make it go deep,
right down to the core,
past seeming, past knowing,
past being me,
where it smelts down all metals,
creating an ore
which is light crushed to weight.
Irradiate
my absence with the final spark
that is my extinction.
Now create
that half-life of speeding
through the seeing dark.

# Flyover Elegies

*(for Jane)*

### I

The traffic's been worse than ever this year,
straining bumper to choking tail,
inching towards the roundabout. We feel
that there's less oxygen to breathe in air,

less room for manoeuvre. Your flyover's arch
holds cars in a rainbow, its pot of gold
somewhere in town. Meanwhile, below,
mothers with pushchairs use the underpass,

struggle with shopping. These are the circles
of Dante's hell. There's the view
from the parapet, of course. But you,
like the transport, wanted somewhere else.

## II

I remember the flyover being built.
The word was for freedom, for rising high
and swiftly, for avoiding a wait.
It was for cruising, for a wider view,
it was for people just passing through.

It sounded like death. All day the pile-
drivers thudded into the earth
with a sickening heartbeat. Flying takes viol-
ence and, the thing is, cement
needs a body before it's a monument.

III

At two in the morning the strongest hug
never touches the hurt. A mug

does something, but delivers less
than a bottle. Now your breath's

part-time, so it disappears,
comes back when you're desperate. Your tears

are diamond earrings. You crave
some rightness, but you don't believe

in anything less than pain: the tug
of concrete, with its credible hug.

IV

I think of you as I'm changing gear,
approaching the junction. In their cars

gilded commuters are longing for home,
profiles pharaonic on the sunset's tomb.

They play radio memories. Illness had made
you less than yourself. I ride

the flyover, clutching the wheel,
in awe of your uninhibited fall

into the streetlights' broken glass.
I envy the gesture but pity the glitz

that has tied up the traffic as your chiffon scarf,
made your belt a roundabout. I feel unsafe

at the apex, not because of despair.
My feet itch, like yours, for the giving air.

# Drought

It needed torching, all that boring moor
above the village. I planted seeds
in several places till the spindly gorse

bore crimson flowers all around its own
of yellow, then collapsed in black.
Borders I planted with exotic blooms

then I watched as arson laid a smoky lawn
as far as the tree line. Beneath its grass
grew a snowdrop season of broken glass.

## Talk with a Headache

I had this headache. Wherever I went
she followed, though I didn't want

her near me. As a hangover she'd lift
quite quickly. But a stab on the left

would start off a migraine, nausea, the lot
so that my darkened room was lit

by aura explosions. Her red-hot vice
was a cap of neuralgia and she wasn't averse

to a little tinnitus thrown in for fun.
I'd try a broadside of Nurofen

but nothing would shift her, not frozen peas,
nor wormwood. I was on my knees,

begging for mercy. 'You've got to see
this is more fun for you than me,

we've got to end it. I'd rather be dead.
I need you like a hole in the head.'

She flinched. I felt her draw softly away,
offended. That week was a holiday

from hurting. Now I was free of her throb
I started to act like a total slob,

ate what I liked – kebabs, very late –
watched trash on the telly, was intimate

with dubious women, didn't hear a peep
from the temples she'd left, never rested up.

But there are some things that are worse than pain.
Soon I felt totally put upon

by a zoo of symptoms, was almost dead
with their chattering inside my head

without my guardian. If you see her round
tell her I'm struggling, want to go to ground

with her for a languorous afternoon
away from myself or I'll go insane

for, though she was clothed in a tiresome ache
she cared for me, had a most healthy take

on all my excesses. She was a wife
to me. And I need her knife.

# Spring

By the time we got back the street had been done
by a bunch of starlings, all of them drunk
and very abusive. I went round the block
three times to avoid them. The local tom

was out on the rampage. The precinct's trees
were growing their leaves like insects again,
a crop of locusts that all wanted in
to the butter-lit rooms. Our diaries

gave hope that the fever of spring and its wounds
would soon be over. No need to ask why
when car-alarm birds called love at the sky.
A fish like a storm cloud swallowed our moon.

# Ménage à Trois

## I *Body*

I sent my body to Bollywood
to become a film star. She wore only beads
draped by the see-through Ganges.

A body unchaperoned by the soul
tends to try everything – some leading men
then, bored with that, occasional women.

She acquired a habit, some discreet tattoos,
married a gangster, went on the game,
had a nervous breakdown. The shame

nearly killed her. I paid the taxi
when she came back. Neighbours strained to see.
Home is the hardest place to be.

## II *Soul*

She was known round here as the woman in white
– an agoraphobic – who ordered in
all her groceries. Considered anodyne

in social circles, this spinster soul
was slowly dying of irony
like a consumption. Her attic eye

was in need of a body to make its way
down to the street – an Antarctic waste
for her, a being who was so chaste

she was abstract, couldn't even blush,
much less know the comfort of sun on her bones,
the joy of a heart attack all of her own.

### III  *Third Party*

But the body's unfaithful and leaves the soul
for another lover. In dishabille
before the doctors, its geometry falls

for a death that wants it, sickness and all.
The grip is erotic – it takes you down
horizontal in your dressing gown,

takes speech, takes memories and then takes breath.
Only then can you feel the humming soul
abandon its story, its particular soil

to rise like a spaceship that has locked its doors
on wondrous technology, unearthly light
which we're forced to forget once it's out of sight.

## Prayer for Bandy

Just because he's dead doesn't mean
that a dog stops guarding.
And as to the question of the canine soul,
I have my opinions.

I held his breath in the palm of my hand,
fresh as a flower. Rest easy now.
He gave us our capacity
for loving him. Original sin

in dogs must be biting. Take pity on him
for being doggy, for not understanding
we don't do that here. We hope
he forgave us for killing him.

Last night, in a dream, he barked at the door.
We opened to three ethereal dogs
who ran to his basket under the stairs
and burnt there, a hearth, as we pulled on our shoes.

## 'One day, feeling hungry'

One day, feeling hungry, I swallowed the moon.
It stuck, like a wafer, to the top of my mouth,
dry as an aspirin. It slowly went down,

showing the gills of my vocal cords,
the folded wings in my abdomen,
the horrible twitch of my insect blood.

Lit from inside, I stood alone
(dark to myself) but could see from afar
the brightness of others who had swallowed stars.

# The Pier

*In memory of Joseph Brodsky*
(1940-1996)

## I

A poet has four bodies.
The Soviet authorities
were too late for the first,
your private polity
which, by now, had chosen democracy
and a funeral parlour
where the credit due
was given entirely to you.
You lay there, an archipelago.

Your wife had the second,
the basic note
against which poets conjugate
the intrigue between things and rhyme,
that murderous love affair with time.
Heart gave you away. Its metronome
was treacherous to you.
Now you don't, but your couplets scan:
you've left all desire to rehearse
the conjugal couplets of deep verse.
Without you, your widow lives in *vers libre*.

The third is your work.
Books perch like birds
in the palms of our open hands and feed
on our attention as we read.
We willingly give your words our breath.

The fourth is your soul.
It left you like a hawk
in search, no doubt, of other work.
Joseph, let snowflakes from its raptor cry
fall back into blankness, till the tip of a tongue
catches one of its crystals, tasting no less
than the terror of nothing more to express.

**II**

Even a healthy heart is lame,
limps its iambic from pillar to post,
with every ventricle pumping the same

flawed syncopation – 'I am, I am.'
Hospital tags are expensive jewellery.
Metre became the cardiogram

you lived by, words at each peak. After all,
each poet is a walk-in heart
filled with world's whooshing. Pause. Then a hall.

## III

The wind on Bangor Pier draws tears
to my eyes as I tread out along each plank,
feeling my usual vertigo
at the strobe of the rucked-up tide below.

You wished me horizon in another place.
I walk out further, each lath of wood
a line of your work that will bear my weight
over the drift of the Menai Straits.

Though absent, you give me solid land.
Six planks to go and I'm out on the edge.
Stamina, you said, is a matter of style.
I find that horizon, grip it like steel.

IV    THE AIR'S GRAFFITI

# Stone Walls

There is an art to seeing through walls.
Old Mícheál had it, as he closed these miles

of Burren pasture. He was a man
whose straightness was in great demand

for he never saw gradient, but would build
right up a cliff face, aiming beyond

for the logical summit. He would place
two boulders together with such poise

that they'd mimic the line of a far-off spur,
rhyming with limestone, making being here

a matter of artistry. I've seen grown men
who scorn the wit of a well-placed dolmen

laugh at his corners, which made visible
the herringbone cast of his rhythmic soul,

his knowledge of water's slant disciplines.
Frost will topple a slapdash cairn

in a season. It takes a humble man to know
gaps matter more in a wall than stone,

making a window on what's really there.
A view, some people. Nothing. Air.

# Woods

Midwinter and this beech wood's mind
is somewhere else. Like fallen light

snow's broken glass fills up the furrows.
Nothing that doesn't have to moves.

We walk through a frozen waterfall
of boles, all held in vertical

except for the careful woodpile laid
in pencils across a tidied glade.

Look back and from the place we were
a bird calls out because we're not there,

a double note whose range expands,
pushing the line where our racket ends

out ever further. That elaborate song
can only exist because we're gone.

A vandal, I shatter that place with a stone.
The bird is for silence. I am for home.

# Red Kites at Tregaron

They know where to find me when they want to feed.
At dusk I prepare, lay out the fat

and spread unspeakable offal in snow
like scarlet necklaces. They know

how to find me. They are my words
for beauty and other birds

fight them, vulgar, down threads of air
which bring them to me. They brawl for hair,

for skin, torn giblets and gizzard which I
provide for them, domestic. Inside

the house is so cold I can see my breath,
my face in the polished oak. My mouth

is sweet with silence. Talon and claw
are tender to me, the craw

much kinder than men. What is most foul
in me kites love. At night I feel

their clear minds stirring in rowan and oak
out in the desert. I stroke

the counterpane, my sleepless skies
filled with the stars of untameable eyes.

## Hermits

I know I could be really good
if I had a private loch and bog
away from the other hermits' cells.
Colman and his bloody bells

disrupt my praying. I can see
his candles burn across the bay
more hours than mine. It drives me wild,
so crowded are these blessèd isles

with would-be saints who all deny
the flesh in more outrageous ways.
I want to be indifferent as stone.
I demand to be holy all on my own.

# Stone Circle

Gladulus is sad.
He stands, a menhir, misunderstood,
lichen covering him like a hood.

He mourns in dolerite. His name's
ironic. When he came,
was planted, a seed at the mercy of time,

he wanted to flower, knew that he could.
Now the surroundings have forgotten the code
to read his story. He is a lode-

stone. He knows his astronomy,
how light slants from a leaden sky
mined by the downpours. Tourists pass by

assuming that he and his circle sleep.
He suffers indignities from sheep
but throbs in the knowledge that sacred shape

has power for ever, whatever's said
from blaspheming tractors. The mad
still hear you. Gladulus, be glad.

# Ancient Aunties

When Gladys put her handbag down
smack in the middle of standing stones
the dancing started. One by one

she touched the boulders, moved like a moon
from granite to sarsen, pacing out praise
for these prominent erections of man,

gliding past the North Pole of her bag
which smelt of lipstick and lavender.
Her pearls became bright satellites of her,

as she moved in ellipses, calling the gods
of darkness and chaos with parabolas
of wonder. No one can say we've gone to the dogs

while modern aunties are still in tune
with ancient eclipses, can stand alone
completing whole families of motionless stone.

# The Mind Museum

## I *The Museum Curator Greets the Dawn*

At nine, I switch on our TV dawn:
the South Wales Transport video game;

Treasures from our Archive (on the blink)
showing some shipwrecks before going blank;

a potted history of the mineral trade
with dotted lines across the world;

and then, my favourite, a timelapse tide
breathing water in weather-wide

and out of the harbour. And then I switch
on haulage engines for the delight

of watching the piston elbows rise and fall.
Precision makes work as musical

as any orchestra. Then I stand
on the model bridge and understand

a museum's museum is being alive.
Quiet please, madam. Yes, we close at five.

Time was they walked on water dry
so full of ships were the teeming docks.
We dream in video what they lived by day.

Masts bobbed like crosses at a crowded quay,
sank from sight inside the gurgling lock.
Time was they walked on water dry.

Men had to travel for a fireman's pay,
they sweated bullets but enjoyed the crack.
We dream in video what they lived by day.

Murmansk, Osaka, Paraguay:
the girls they met there call them back...
Time was they walked on water dry,

met Welshmen everywhere, and lay
by stanchions up some Godforsaken creeks.
We dream in video what they lived by day.

Back home in Cardiff, hear the halyards play
sweet music when the winds fall slack.
Time was they walked on water dry.
We dream in video what they lived by day.

### III  *Website Future*

No need for me once we're on the net,
are a wave to be surfed on, have gone world-wide.
No awkward engines to curate
but templates which never knew a tide.

And if TV signals are never lost
but flare round the world until a mind
receives them, then surely this e-mail will last
much longer than paper. Fast-forward, rewind

are history. Let the servers serve
their megabyte karma in encoded air.
Long live the roll of the mouse, the curve
of choices made when I won't be here.

Then nobody'll tell us where we've just been
but we'll make our own history, piece by piece,
be free to improvise and glean
our version, far from chronicle police.

But on monitors the bands of rain
sweep in, interference on our charts.
Remember the real matters more than the known.
Unforecast snow falls softly in our hearts.

## IV  *Communications*

I phoned him from a standing stone
to prove to him that I was still there.
And I was worshipful:
granite, horizon, message, air.

I called him from a holy well
hoping for miracles, a cure.
My prayers cost dearly in time
and candles. But he didn't care.

I dialled via satellite.
I needed an answer to my despair.
I got it. *Sorry, we can't connect you.*
*Please try again later. Nobody here.*

## V *On Duty*

First things first: the Crossword of the Day,
which I do while showing visitors the way.

I'm paid for boredom and the tide
of non-events on which I ride.

We're waiting to hear about our jobs.
Six across could be the *Ace of Spades.*

What would I curate if I had to leave?
These mud flats? *Anagram: Reprieve.*

The open handbag of a screaming gull?
The passing clouds? *Fifteen is Dull.*

The crossword setter, my anonymous friend
gives me clues to my unknown mind.

These are snakes and ladders you'll never climb
or follow to anywhere. Last word is *Time.*

## VI  *Night Galleries*

Maybe today they'll change the tapes!
It's the same old stories – first there was steam,
steel, then depression, then developed bay –
stories so fixed I can never say
more than they let me. At night I dream

these galleries shift. We open screens,
show new exhibits. The best one's my heart
in a glass case and it switches on
and off like a light bulb. This intimate room
is floodlit, is a work of art. Stop, start. Stop, start. Stop, start.

## Will and the Wall

'Well!' said Will to the wall,
but the wall said nothing at all to Will.

*

'Forsooth!' The Count of Monte Cristo eyed his cell
with calculation. He'd heard the tapping,
had decided escape was a matter of style

and special attention. No mortar could withstand his stare.
Nothing would love him as much again
as the wall he seduced, that became his door.

*

When pushed, the wall said 'Nothing' to Will
who, shocked, could only manage a 'Well!'

*

*Kerrunch!* Now *that's* talking.
A cartoon cat
is a concertina played by a fall
and hitting top C. It's broom-handle
heart attack, *yoiks!* and *kerpow!*
It's saying: fantasy's all very well,
you may *think* you're an arrow
but a wall's in the way
and the literal's stronger, remember.
*Splatt!* Now.

*

Once it had started to talk, the wall
couldn't stop itself. Will listened well.

*

And overnight these words appeared
in day-glo spray paint:
     *PC Evans is a sad man.*
     *PC Davies needs a vasectomy*
and this on the station. Now I know
I'm just a cleaner, but stones cry out
their truthfulness. I'm paid
to hush them. Best thing is, my fee
doesn't cover insistence. See, the next day
it's *Evans* who *needs a vasectomy*
and *D. is a pansy.*
Nothing at all to do with me,
but there's gold in them graffiti.

*

In winter the crack let in the slugs
and sky to the kitchen. The garden looked lush
through the chink, less slum
than tropical. Mysterious glair
jazzed up the carpets. The slugs themselves,
of course, were never there.

*

Well, thingummy, thingummy Will tum wall.
Ti tum wall thingummy thingummy Will.

*

Been swimming so long this water's a wall
that I can see through.
Kick, tumble turn and breathe,
pulling so fast that I'm standing still.
Repeat it all as before and turn.
Bricked up inside this barricade
I'm climbing swiftly on liquid ropes
but going nowhere. Don't look down
in case I remember the air and drown.

*

And all was well between Will and the wall,
so we all came to sit and stare with Will.

*

When I die I shall bequeath a wall
to this village so all the kids with their balls
can do rebound practice. What else is there to do
out in the country? I'll site it carefully,
away from the houses, so the structure can ring
with ricochet, swoop, reverse catch and swing
and kids will play on when the adults' eyes
have lost sight of the grid for which all aim
on summer evenings. In time their game
will become its own end and, piece by piece,
will dismantle the inner carapace
that has kept their souls from the wider view
not behind my memorial wall but through
its structure. Balls bounce back
at predictable angles, thoughts recoil
at the barricade's blankness, an inner door
swings open. All you have to do is stare
for long enough and everything's there.

# The Flaggy Shore

*(for Nora Nolan)*

Even before I've left, I long
for this place. For hay brought in before the rain,
its stooks like stanzas, for glossy cormorants
that make metal eyes and dive like hooks,
fastening the bodice of the folding tide
which unravels in gardens of carraigín.
I walk with the ladies who throw stones at the surge
and their problems, don't answer the phone
in the ringing kiosk. Look. In the clouds
hang pewter promontories, long bays
whose wind-indented silent coasts
make me homesick for where I've not been.
Quicksilver headlands shoot into the night
till distance and the dying of day
dull steel and vermilion to simple lead
blown downwind to the dark, then out of sight.